SEASON OF VIOLENCE

By the same author:

Poetry:

It's About Time
Hottentot Venus
Appollo Cafe and Other Poems
Penguin Book of Southern African Verse (ed.)

Fiction:

John Ross: The True Story
Born of Man
Time of Our Darkness
War Child

Criticism:

Southern African Literature: An Introduction

Stephen Gray

SEASON OF VIOLENCE

Dangaroo  Press

Acknowledgements

To the editors of the following publications where some of these poems first appeared, with gratitude: *London Review of Books* ('Letter'), *PN Review* ('The Venice Connection'), *Meanjin* ('Resistance', 'Liberal Feature', 'Between Men'), *New Contrast* ('Returnees', 'Proposition'), *New Coin* ('The Thing Is'), *English Academy Review* ('Last to Go') and *Kunapipi* ('Season of Violence', 'Returnees').

Cover painting by Norman Catherine, 'Martyr' (1991), oil on canvas, 200 x 152 cms., by courtesy of the artist and the Johannesburg Art Gallery.

First published in 1992 by Dangaroo Press
Australia: G.P.O. Box 1209, Sydney, New South Wales, 2001
Denmark: Pinds Hus, Geding Søvej 21, 8381 Mundelstrup
UK: 80 Kensington Road, Earlsdon, Coventry CV5 6GH

ISBN 1 871049 87 3
Printed in Great Britain by Villiers Publications, London N6

For Anna and Kirsten

Contents

Season of Violence

has not ended; was due to close;
termination was fully announced –
prayer-day now throughout the nations –

the air is cluttered with silent words –
can't breathe for ascending petitions;
not over yet; only begun

a derailment at Mariannhill;
Sunday is another killer in South Africa;
take a philosophical view:

'O Lord afford me detachment
from those who want to but don't know how;
bullets through flesh fly easily'

As Archbishop Tutu said Martin Luther
King said: 'those who live an eye
for an eye end up blind people'

will not end; for ever and ever;
help out now; Amen.

After the Emergency

Cauterised; the sensors in the brain
are disconnected from the human web,
the best part has been shock-treated out

one for his sins now retreats
despite the boycott and the time-death
to render Japanese or Provencal

another flies out of the morass
of crumbled letters and bent figures
a preassembled technicolour kite

a third exiles himself on the beach
voyeuring the strip of male muses
peeling velcro down impossible flanks

so: scar-tissue holds the lost memory
at least, nerve-ends may still be intertwined;
knot them; restructure node by node

the wholeness of a rime, the inter-
view that stretches from here forth,
include; hold; recover all:
make the country and its poets new.

Returnees

on their knees touch soil
a generation lost and found

frame time again and
focus on the true subject

bring expertise and vocabulary
from another world apart

apply themselves to pulling closed
the chasm between their and our lives

the great rift will soon entomb
their and our past, level all

renegotiating exile they face
privately the force of their desertion.

Conventional Wisdom

The lay of the land is given
Resources are naturally people

The emperor may not change his clothes
There's no sense in complaining

Iron-fisted policies quash
Thin out the pickets with poison

Shoot your antagonist in the rear
Shred the files before enquiry:

The poet shreds grammar shoots
Round corners clutches banners

Holds the pen in padded flesh
Makes this complaint: No clothes!

His only resource is in the mouths of men,
Sings at burials which change the land.

Funeral in Soweto

Amo a mass a machet
a machine-gun... a massacre

I love you love he/she/
it loves we love you (plural)

they love in all their persons
actively in their present:

a moment amass a mattress
(first lesson: basic conjugation)

we love you they love
a machet a martyr a manacle

(a morgue of taxi-drivers train
passengers loved ones).

Down to Zero

Iron-fisted weather: crackdown
on outdoor gatherings curfew road-blocks

(is this the only way they know?)
the last people they trust are poets –
variable coming in from the south –

night-walks are forbidden while the trains
are ridden by red-bandanaed armies:

dispersing the people – nature's police-
man drives them home to burning shacks:
the agony is people have no place to go

gone shopping gone to church no place
to which to return in inclement weather
(there is no home for 5 million people)

(is that all they know: bring down
the thunder and guns, the tyretracks
and chains, the hail, the snow?)

poets are in *their* ghettoes, too:
make shelters grow while zero is reached.

Resistance

The peace march to old Mayfair
Recreation Hall is legal now

– the golden banners furl up Central
young democrats of honour

but as they assemble they're warned:
brick through the fanlight

speakers of policy evacuate
before the smaller groups

if one is picked off by a cruising Kombi
they split like shrapnel

if one is killed they bear the news
all night the right-wing stalk

the streets and alleys armed
and when their quarry's home

plant bombs that blow the
thousand plates of glass out

in the frigid air at two a.m.
(my cafe had its wall removed)

welcome the new South African season
to complain of armed men is treason

(Costa and Audrey scoop the sugar
up in bursting litter-bags)

All in All

Taken as a whole
he's responsive loving
dependent on circumstances:

feed him warm him bed him
you get the best result:
total attention to detail

no food no heat no linen
you still have this metonymy
a part'll arouse and spit

though affording him small pleasure
and much pain to you
the mechanism's automatic

drive him out ill and lonely
the cold hand of death's
his last live frisson

when the revolution fails
the pay-off to the masses
this last kick is theirs:

fists raised deliver stones
for spent casings:
pleasure beyond recollection.

These Days

Some children are playing Prokofiev
while others are loose in the streets

rioting uneducated starved neglected

yes, comrades – no party can bring 'em all in
doubling themselves for the millennium –

the National Youth Orchestra
plays Prokofiev's third piano

and brittle sticky music like machines

carries their cocky soloist

swoops in soupy syncopation

what in Chicago 1921 all
the adults could hardly get their ears to –

dazzling toccata, theme with variations...

the future's definitely in their hands.

The Thing Is

there are no mercies left
in the shameless ruthless land

'beloved country' past crying
the white milk over dark skin is spilt

the body count rises: this month's 137
unidentified corpses to be burnt on Tuesday –

claim your dead, the dead spilt
on my rocky bosom (vide Schreiner)

at least in her day she knew who they were
at least old Paton could label each cut down

these human torches have no names:
fuel for the flames.

Tyranny of Knives

for cutting bread not bodies
tomatoes, not sunk into my heart

having escaped knives narrowly
I am not fond of them
the damage they may do
out of the kitchen rack
pressed against my skin

take your weapons and throw them in the sea,
said the sage of disarmament

take this blade from my artery
if now my neck is slit
how do you intend to use me?
I shall not be able to assist
in your vandalous activity

there are other voices I would hear
a while longer of those I love:
not shut-up, give me –
no, you give me my life,
it's at the point of your knife
do not press.

Letter

I go out to post a letter get gunned down
To purchase milk in a bottle get gunned down

Go to the festival in Fordsburg to see a film
About Langston get a bomb thrown at me

Take a taxi from Bok Street with a dozen
Others get picked off arbitrarily

Squat on the banks of Benoni
Get shack raised skull stoved

Take the Soweto train get evicted
Before New Canada by vigilantes

Clubbed by police necklaced
And ridden over by an Armskor Buffalo

I go to make my complaint at Union Building
Get mugged on the lawn left for dead

Dead me do not speak so what can I say?
This letter will have to do:

I go out to post a letter get gunned down
Get gunned down.

Taken as Read

The question's post-theoretical:
know the baby by its birthmarks,
prating Engels, studied Stalin
(indeed he was my first nightmare);
Saussurely Derridaed, you learnt Foucault,
but loved to wallow in Barthes,
he signified the empire of your style;
a Jung man, you held a line
through Prattfalls and the feminist,
unconscious of *Love's Body* and Marcuse;
hard to teach an ageing dog tricks:
structuring, that was it, at your post –
the great debate in triplicate –
letting the adult stand (or fall)
by all this wisdom second-hand:
strike up the banned then,
publish all your hidden heresies;
this game only converts if you master it:
all right, so – what's new, South Africa?
that's my allegiance... and yours?
mine is the perpetual sentence of syntax,
the nail in the coffin that full stops.

Eight o'Clock News

The Minister said:
the omelette cannot be unscrambled now,
constituent cheese from tomato
or diced ham from chopped onion,
still less the autonomous yolk
from the white in which it free-floated,
they've all flavoured together
over the simmering flame

He has now turned this dish over
to check that it isn't half-baked

(one history, economy and vote)
those who cooked up this recipe
had homelands for cows and for pigs
and for veggies in rural areas
and batteries apart for productive chickens

(but it's all one national enterprise now –
the united omelette of new South Africa)
but what the Minister didn't say
regarding this transcendental omelette –
knife and fork poised over its puckered skin,
as in a sacrament breaking it forth
all over again into gorgeable bites –
is who apart from his eminent self
gets to swallow the wretched thing.

Liberal Feature

African Jim, passed by the British Board of Censors
for general viewing (signed Harlech),
reveals in black and white the first native –

call him Jim the Million, restless in his Swazi kraal
waves his ruralite savages off
a waggon a bus a train to the wicked city

of pulsing Jazz Maniacs
mugged by his own kind a good boss-boy takes him in
they sing about this: natural harmony

as a singing waiter in a night-club shebeen
Jim takes Dolly's heart by the arm, walks her
through gang-infested slums crooning

the caption says it all: simple people
Jim can make the blues sound happy
he neither eats drinks cries for his beloved country

show your teeth Jim (whatever your name is)
on celluloid you do survive –
show the Queen: how natural's your rhythm?

Robinson's Parrot

Pretty Polly, Pretty Polly!
Stop that senseless chatter!
Such bea-utiful feathers...
Rise 'n shine, Robinson

Climb on my shoulder, there's a good girl...
Monarch of all I survey, qua qua
– Came on a wave and took you as slave –
Clipped your wings, flighty thing

Pull out these weeds, clear those trees!
Say you love me, Friday...
Keep your filthy hands off her, she's mine!
Qua qua, faa-rk you!

Taught you your two plus two...
What about my soul, Polly?
Have another bloody banana!
Let me out of this faa-rking cage!

I don't understand a word you say
I am your recording device
I'll outlive you, qua qua...
I am immortal.

Family Photos

The backgrounds speak more:
younger head and shoulders against
old church facades/bridges/
slopes/rockeries/fountains
for one second thought to be
suitably picturesque/memorable

now do I know the countries/
dates/traditional spots?
Unusual holidays: creeping snow
for people who wear hats against sun,
water features for the dried-out,
crumbling old bodyworks for
these tourists from a new land.

And especially cars/trains/
boats signalling severance...
the faces before (hair combed/
bag or fist held correctly,
stomachs in, shoulders back)
ingrained in hope against
such an always similar world.

Last to Go

Trained near Mexico as a fruit-grower,
With a Spanish name and a You-Bet accent;

On assisted passage to Durban and from a rattling truck
He staked out a slope of bush near Nelspruit;

Purty soon with the locals inspanned:
Orchards for thorn-trees and ant-hills into pawpaws;

Caraceto he named his plot, in remembrance
Of the U.S. frontier cleared across here too;

Skin cancer got him, so with his wife and capital
He pioneered forests on the cooler escarpment;

Under Finnish pines in his long retirement
He fished with old flies the trout in others' streams;

Deaf, blind, incontinent, he sat like a stump,
Poaching by feel the fingerlings he'd put in there first;

And he'd played a wicked game of rummy;
The last of the old brigade, You-Bet.

Welcome

Do you understand when I say Come In
I mean all of you into my parlour

And Hold on a Sec I mean touch me
Let your fingertips take my wrist

Wait a Mo means lock your eyes on mine
But are you Sure? raise them in question

For Good to See You read Ah Blue-eyes
How're you Doing? who've you been with?

Let's Take this Another Way means
Unbutton yourself let it all hang out...

When I conclude Come Again Some Time
Believe me I mean more than I say

This is the point: phatic language
No longer clasps my situation

Without desiring touch foolish noise
Hands insert best: See Ya.

Proposition

In those former days to say I loved you
meant I depended on you to alter my life

this did not happen: disturbance there was
but no matter how we tried no break occurred

I must thank you for trying to change me
God knows it cost you, before you left

somehow over time that difference took place
call it molecular arrangements their own code

there was no straight trajectory I have grown
apart from what I was destined to be

now love as an active agent is gone
I find I love you all the more

without conditions or expectations without
promises even or intentions, but: firmly.

Therefore I propose we try this new bond
see this time about your deeper structure.

Intermission

Why don't I make the coffee
While you make your debate?

Stop the hands fluttering
Get a fix on caffeine

The oil of the blend
Stimulates your reply

Until the kettle's boiled
Fight this negative thing off

Plunge out the impure grains
Water as solvent, the medium

At the prospect you're more focused
How did you say you take it?

This'll keep you rigid and alert
One night can be decisive.

Red Roses

What is it about this great display?
The dome that opens if you watch?

The colour of old bedclothes unfurling?
Where a fingertip probes soft red?

Is it the sweet hollow that evaporates?
The prickles of the thrusting stem?

Speaking for itself, heads for light?
Out of the drought peels back petals?

Is easily blown, becomes spent?
Cannot renew itself but via the roots?

To question a long language I have cut
A rising dozen red roses for you.

I present them, my interrogation done:
Now you tell me, what does this mean?

Between Men

an intimacy that has not to do
with the exclusion of others –

the cooking and cleaning of homes,
the breakage of older relationships –

this refuge of like-minded middle age
when before the next one career is done

this sporty drinking solidarity
an adhesion that stops the drift:

playing cards until midnight past,
jack on queen and queen on king –

jokers turn up – the suited hierarchy
works a familiar world of regular values –

this is known to be merely a game;
outside the rules are changed; your turn.

Lyric Impulse

My dear Nadezhda, Today the impulse
that wells from deeper than I know
flooded my hand and calm mind
knowing where it had to be led

– I do not know whose it is
nor from where it comes...
only that if I am in the perfect state
inspiration can be relied upon –

under this spell I worked
from 9.00 until 3.05
missing tea and lunch
writing out fast and nimbly
as I've learnt to when inspired

until the postman disturbed me
(with your welcome cheque)
or my ink ran dry or many
other interventions. If I work at it
tomorrow the outpouring will resume.
Love, Tchaikovsky.

The Herb Garden

My mother before she died insisted
I should have a herb garden
Something in her English soul
Amid rough South Africans
Called for the tenderness of mint
The old scent of lavender and sage

They arrived in soggy pages of *The Star*
With a spade taller than herself
She dug them into my backyard
Before I was ready for them
A cigarette tightly in her lips
Explaining chives made life worthwhile

That is how she died in her own
Garden of sweet remembrance
Very frail then with a bucket and spade
The size we children used for play
Always finding the sun too hot the soil
Far too dry for the gentler herbs

Today after the long heart-stopping drought
My mother's bed of lost spices
Has so flourished I have to cut it back
And the mint is in the crevices of fingers
The sage under my very nails
And I remember her every gesture.

Ballpen on Paper

This liberation is taking too long:
Dumile Feni, born on May Day, 42,
draws his way from the backveld,
intense his subjects, there is terror
at work on the heads, hands expressed,
the fear of breaking with pain back
into dumb bleeding lost herds

discriminated from the salons, the galleries,
disqualified as an artist, endorsed out,
the only route into exile he took,
by 1968 he was gone from our midst
– hook the man in a butcher's
coolroom by the wrist, let him
be free in New York for decades to express himself

but then, Dumile, the heart is supposed
to warm and the door to creak an inch –
you almost made it back, to open
the show of your younger self,
now the 'national treasure' of our
rediscovered, heartless, wicked past,
died by seizure the day before,

these sentences were just too long,
the reconciliation was too postponed
for one human being to bear:
you leave us not your fine art
at rest on the wall – ballpen on paper –
where it may be read as a warning
but your agony in the streets
climbing way out of the frame.

Bring Out Your Dead

He predicts no poems during plague
as the wave reaches south
by 95 and peaks at 21%
total harvest: bring 'em out
bring 'em out... mostly blacks,
women and children first... unrest causes
(read civil war) families to break
and who migrates and sleeps around most?
At all times fill the teat of this
rubber good with your burning sperm.
Employment's to be had in wards
and morgues, the low dress the lost.
An epidemic virus makes us kin
as nothing more humane has done:
the salt of tears in which we swim,
saliva as we kiss, the banks of
bottled blood may each contain
the thump and urge of level death:
bring out your dead that we may see
how each of us may risk and only lose,
figures indicate survivors positively are
an altogether sweeter people.

Lunchbreak

Between the signing and the wining
Comes the routine lunch

He will not take calls
Till two or three or four

Beneath his feet the watchman
Who keeps much stricter hours

Opens a curried take-away
With his fingers on the floor.

Closed on Mondays

Yes, this is the room where I work –
my space with books up the wall
never the way one designed
but in progress my productivity

three desks for beginning, middle
and end – shelves for the shelved
correspondence is urgent less urgent
and the time for Christmas cards
may pass again unmarked on calendars

closed on Mondays: I hold my stayaway
phone unplugged pen screwed up
unopened pad text arrested
workers may protest the unjust tax
the government take on all the writer makes

closed like a museum or other institution
open on Tuesday at nine
for you to pay now, step up and pay.

Children of Ra

Original title: The Economy of Nature
or, The Grand Hymn to Ra
attributed to Akhenaton, B.C. 1372
whose wife we know, Nefertiti
and son-in-law Tutankhamen,
the master of pharaonic glyphs
(freely translated from a version in French):
'How very numerous the things you have created
Even those deeply hidden from view
O Unique God above Whom is no other,
The universe you have created following your heart,
Remaining alone:
All things, men, herds and savage beasts,
All those on earth who walk on paws and on feet,
Those who climb and may sail on their wings,
All of Egypt and its hinterland;
You have made each person in place and foreseen his needs,
Each to his nourishment, the length of his life counted,
Divided by languages of different expression,
Since you have cut us off from strangers
Our characters like our skins are distinct,
Remaining alone:
Cities, districts, fields, highways, rivers,
But you are the disc of day over the earth.'

For the Middle Dynasty this was a fine manoeuvre,
one Sun-God, monotheism for all,
the obviously superior lonely power
that made mud crawl, fruit seed,
such obvious glory to strike all living things;
post-empire stuff really, the union of the gods,
God is for a business-like religion and the pyramids
he had built with untold labour
on deserts in the plain light of day,
his arrogance to reach his God first,

King of Upper and Lower and all other Egypts,
Akhenaton the Heretic after whom
the lowly lapsed into rivalries anon.

The Venice Connection

How can I make notes about your much written-over
city? co-opted in my language by Byron through James –

once through the lanes of the old Venetian Republic
you said No one has babies; we're growing old, dying –

part of my Grand Tour and late education I have had
  advantage
of your walk-in history, your prosecco, your unforgivable
  colours –

and much of my heart has remained in your generous flat
round the clock-tower through stalls off Saint Mark's Square,
  heavens!

hearing your voice on the phone is always a return
yet again, how intimately I know your blunt inflections, your
  tone –

nothing of our life here is Venetian: no past that isn't
  suppressed,
no water to make us kin, no procession from the ghetto to the
  tombs –

the palimpsest to peel back from the blueprint is missing,
here everyone's young and knows less and less –

I would take as my heritage your days of slavery, too,
and if I could paint, paint crowdedly down to the household
  dog –

inclusive panoramas and yes if you want, God Himself on
  high,
although on that score I remain as deeply disbelieving as
  you –

40

they've a Bridge of Sighs here from one concrete bunker
to the next where prisoners march, but that is the only
  connection –

old merchant, my friend, only this in reply to your tongue:
my greetings, my love always, teach me your staying-power.

Stephen Gray was born in South Africa in 1941 and graduated from Cambridge and the Iowa Workshop. His first volume, *It's About Time*, appeared in Cape Town in 1974, followed by *Hottentot Venus* (London, 1979) and *Love Poems, Hate Poems* (London, 1982). His *Apollo Café and Other Poems (1982-89)* was published by David Philip in Cape Town, with whom he is preparing his *Selected Poems*. He has edited the *Penguin Book of Southern African Verse* (1989). He is also known as a novelist and lives and works in Johannesburg.

Stephen Gray. Photo: Michael Dunne